I0417959

*"The books you read and the people
you associate with will determine
what you accomplish in life."*

Gracen Gonzalez

What Top Achievers Who Know Gracen Have to Say about Him

"Gracen is one of the very top students I've worked with in my decades-long education career. He has created many STEM projects, has the heart of an engineer, and is a young man of outstanding character."

Colonel Mark Hyatt
USAF (ret.) - Former Director of the USAFA Center for Character and Leadership Development

"Gracen is mentally rugged, physically strong, intellectually focused, and deeply passionate about his dreams of attending the USAFA and the contribution he'd like to make to the world. It's rare for a young person to possess such a clear, and consistent vision for themselves and then work towards that dream at such a high level and with such passion and consistency."

Bruce Babashan
USA Boxing & Pro Boxing Trainer

"There are certain people who you know are going to do big things in the world. They have a unique mixture of intelligence, character, personality, and grit. Gracen Gonzalez is one of those few."

Jim Harshaw Jr.
NCAA Division I Wrestling Coach
and All American Wrestler

"I have known Gracen since he was 8. I have never met a more driven, talented, and intelligent young man. He has a passion for a myriad of intellectual, artistic, and athletic pursuits and excels at all of them. I have thoroughly enjoyed watching him grow into an exceptional young man and leader. His acceptance into the US Air Force Academy and subsequent service will make this country safer."

Brad Coughlin - Major US Army (Ret)
Army Ranger, Special Forces Medic, and Medical Officer

Launch Pad

Mitchell, Doolittle, Yeager, Patton
and the Quest for Leadership
and Success Wisdom

by Gracen Gonzalez
with Ruben Gonzalez

Olympia
Press

This publication is designed to provide accurate and authoritative information in regard to the subject matter covered. It is sold with the understanding that the publisher is not engaged in rendering legal, accounting or other professional service. If legal advice or other expert assistance is required, the services of a competent professional should be sought.

Olympia Press
832-689-8282

Ordeting Information
Quantity sales. Special discounts are available on quantity purchases by corporations, associations and others. For details, call 832-689-8282 Individual sales. Olympia Press publications are available through most bookstores. They can also be ordered directly from Olympia Press. Orders for college textbook/course adoption use. Please contact the publisher.

Library of Congress Cataloging-in-Publication Data

Gonzalez, Gracen
  Launch Pad: Mitchell, Doolittle, Yeager, Patton and the quest for leadership and success wisdom / Gracen Gonzalez and Ruben Gonzalez
      p. cm.
ISBN: 979-8-9865188-1-7
1. Leadership. 2. Success-Psychological aspects. I. Title
HF5388.B888 2022
658.4'000-dc21

Printed in the United States of America

10 9 8 7 6 5 4 3

To Mom and Dad:
Thank you for your love,
encouragement, challenge and prayers.
I'm proud to be your son.

How this Book Came to Be
by Ruben Gonzalez

Ever since an early age Gracen loved building and flying planes—from ultralight competitive rubber-band-powered balsa planes that flew for over two minutes to self-designed and built-from-scratch remote control planes.

When Gracen was 10 years old, and needed a way to fund his hobby, I told him that every time he read a personal development book and wrote a list of the lessons he learned from it, I would pay him $10.

Over the next couple of years Gracen read over 80 books.

He's been applying what he learned ever since. The results speak for themselves. Gracen is a top student, two-time Colorado State Judo Champion, captain of his high school wrestling team, he owns a 3D printing business, and he's an award-winning piano player.

Gracen always wanted to write a book so we decided to take some of the things he learned from his favorite books and share them here, so that more people will start reading personal development books to better themselves.

Launch Pad is filled with tips from Gracen's favorite history, leadership, teamwork, success and free enterprise books.

I hope that some of the things you learn here will help you achieve your goals as well.

Ruben Gonzalez
Colorado Springs 2022

Introduction

by Gracen Gonzalez

I'm 17 and live in Colorado Springs, Colorado. I've always loved aviation and engineering. When I was 10, I started building and flying planes. I soloed at the age of 16 and am currently pursuing my pilots license. I wrestle for Palmer Ridge High School, and I own a 3D printing and design business that sells high quality engineering models.

My dream is to study mechanical or aeronautical engineering at the U.S. Air Force Academy. I see attending the Air Force Academy as the best way to improve myself and serve my country.

I always wanted to write a book. In *Launch Pad*, I share some of the things that I learned from reading over 80 personal development books — how to dream big, to always pursue your dreams, to push through no matter what, and much, much more.

I've chosen some of my favorite books and I'm sharing just enough to hopefully get you to read some of them as well. I hope *Launch Pad* helps you set a positive trajectory to your dreams!

Gracen Gonzalez
Colorado Springs, CO

LaunchPadGracen.com

Contents

Part Three - Teamwork

Part Four - Success Principles

Part Five - Free Enterprise

Part One

Lessons from History

The Wright Brothers

by David McCullough

This is the story about the courageous brothers who showed the world how to fly —Wilbur and Orville Wright.

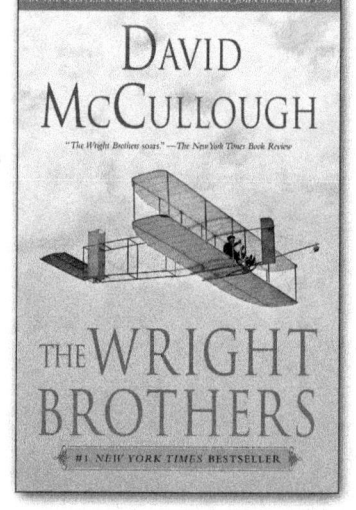

In 1903 in Kitty Hawk, North Carolina, two brothers, bicycle mechanics from Dayton, Ohio, changed history.

The Wright brothers were men of courage and determination. They also had far-ranging interests and deep curiosity. They complemented each other perfectly. Wilbur was an analytical thinker, while Orville was a mechanical whiz. When they worked together, nothing seemed impossible.

This biography helps appreciate aviation and teamwork.

Lessons and Takeaways

"If we worked on the assumption that what is accepted as true really is true, then there would be little hope for advance."

"With all the knowledge and skill acquired in thousands of flights in the last ten years, I would hardly think today of making my first flight on a strange machine in a twenty-seven-mile wind, even if I knew that the machine had already been flown and was safe."

Wilbur Wright

"We were lucky enough to grow up in a home where we were always encouraged to pursue our intellectual interests; to investigate whatever aroused our curiosity."

"If birds can glide for long periods of time, then... why can't we?"

"Isn't it astonishing that all these secrets have been preserved for so many years just so we could discover them!"

Billy Mitchell

by Alfred Hurley

Billy Mitchell was the father of the US Air Force. He was one of the most influential people in the 20th century.

While serving in France during WWI, he saw the potential of aviation as a military force and was willing to fight for his beliefs in convincing the U.S. Army to embrace aviation.

Mitchell faced huge opposition and was even court-martialed for insubordination because he voiced his beliefs so passionately.

Without Mitchell's warning, the United States might never have been able to build up the world's largest air force in time to fight World War II.

Lessons and Takeaways

If you are passionate about something, stick to your guns. To be a genius is to be misunderstood.

Nothing can stop the attack of aircraft except other aircraft.

Progress is never accepted by everybody.

The world stands on the threshold of the "aeronautical era." During this epoch the destinies of all people will be controlled through the air.

Changes in military systems come about only through the pressure of public opinion or disaster in war.

"Our nation's future is indissolubly bound up in the development of air power."

Billy Mitchell

Hap Arnold
by Bill Yenne

General Henry "Hap" Arnold was an American aviation pioneer.

He was a strong supporter of Billy Mitchell's attempt to create an independent Air Force. He believed fighters should be used to attack, not only to protect bombers. He encouraged the development of the B-17 Flying Fortress. Which was a bomber capable of defending itself.

He was also the first five-star general of the U.S. Air Force, the first American to carry air mail, and the person responsible for the war-winning air strategy of World War Two.

Lessons and Takeaways

"Your limits are somewhere up there, waiting for you to reach beyond infinity."

"A modern, autonomous, and thoroughly trained Air Force, at all times will not alone be sufficient, but without it, there can be no national security."

"Offense is the essence of air power."

"As a nation we were not prepared for World War II. Yes, we won the war, but at a terrific cost in lives, human suffering, and material, and at times the margin was narrow. History alone can reveal how many turning points there were, how many times we were near losing, and how our enemies' mistakes pulled us through. In the flush of victory, some like to forget these unpalatable truths."

"A second-best air force is like a second best hand in poker—it's no good at all."

Hap Arnold

The Boys Who Challenged Hitler

by Phillip Hoose

Denmark didn't resist the German occupation at the beginning of World War II. Ashamed of their cowardly leaders, a small group of Danish boys decided to take action against the Nazis.

They formed the secret Churchill Club to resist the German occupation. They destroyed and sabotaged German equipment for six months until they were tracked down and arrested.

They became national heroes and inspired the Danish resistance.

After the war, Churchill personally honored their courage and actions.

Lessons and Takeaways

Have the courage to do what you can with what you have right now.

The boys had the courage to start doing small things to show opposition to Hitler. As they gained experience, they were able to perform more difficult missions.

If you don't like something,
don't just complain—do something about it.

Think ahead. The rules of the Churchill Club show that the boys understood that what they were doing was very dangerous. They had thought about the consequences if they were caught.

When starting a big project, think about the consequences of your actions. If you decide the reward is worth the risk, commit 100% to taking consistent action.

I Could Never be So Lucky Again

by Jimmy Doolittle

General Doolittle was involved in every phase of aviation from barnstormers to WWII jets. An aeronautical engineer and a pioneer of modern aviation technology, he was the first pilot to fly across the U.S. in under 24 hours.

He organized and led the air raid over Tokyo in WWII, the first American attack on the Japanese mainland. The attach was a psychological blow for the Japanese.

Jimmy Doolittle was bold and courageous. He wasn't lucky; he made his own luck. He was willing to try different things and challenge old ways of thinking. By doing so, he helped change the world.

Lessons and Takeaways

"Try to make the world a better place for your having been here."

"You can't lose a war if you have command of the air, and you can't win a war if you haven't."

"Worry about those things you can fix. If you can't fix it, don't worry about it; accept it and do the best you can."

"Think! Use your head! If we have to fight, we should be prepared to do so from the neck up instead of from the neck down."

Jimmy Doolittle

"To become an ace, a fighter must have extraordinary eyesight, strength, agility, a huntsman's eye, coolness in a pinch, calculated recklessness, a full measure of courage, and occasional luck!"

Flags of Our Fathers

by James Bradley

James Bradley was the son of one of the Marines who raised the flag at Iwo Jima.

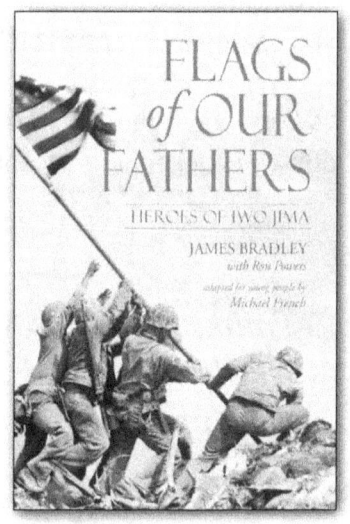

This book is the story of the six men who raised the flag and their part in the battle for the Pacific's most crucial island.

The most interesting part of this story is what happened to the six men after the battle.

This book helps you understand the meaning of being a hero.

Lessons and Takeaways

"Roughly fifty percent of procedure in a Marine basic-training program is about disconnecting the young American boy from his concept of himself as a unique individual, a lone operator."

"Use it up, wear it out, make it do, or do without."

"When I asked him, fifty-three years after the event, 'Mr. Lucas, why did you jump on those grenades?' he did not hesitate with his answer: 'To save my buddies.'"

"That is how we always keep our beloved dead alive, isn't it? By telling stories about them; true stories."

"Today, the word 'hero' is often confused with 'celebrity.' Celebrities seek fame; they take action to get attention. Heroes are heroes because they have risked something to help others. Their actions involve courage."

James Bradley

Yeager

by Chuck Yeager

General Chuck Yeager was the first man to fly faster than the speed of sound. He was a World War II flying ace, and h e s h o t d o w n a Messerschmitt jet with a prop-driven P-51 Mustang.

This is Yeager's story of what it was like to dogfight over Nazi Europe, how he escaped after being shot down over occupied France, and how he was able to break the sound barrier a few days after cracking his ribs in a horse-riding accident.

This book helps you understand what you can do if you settle for nothing less than excellence.

Lessons and Takeaways

"At the moment of truth, there are either reasons or results."

"If you can walk away from a landing, it's a good landing. If you use the airplane the next day, it's an outstanding landing."

"I was always afraid of dying. Always. It was my fear that made me learn everything I could about my airplane and my emergency equipment and kept me flying respectful of my machine and always alert in the cockpit."

"The best pilots fly more than the others; that's why they're the best."

Chuck Yeager

"If you want to grow old as a pilot, you've got to know when to push it and when to back off."

"You do what you can for as long as you can, and when you finally can't, you do the next best thing: you back up, but you don't give up."

"You don't concentrate on risks; you concentrate on results. No risk is too great to prevent the necessary job from getting done."

Part Two

Leadership

General Patton's Leadership Principles
by Porter Williamson

General Patton led the Allied invasion of Sicily in WWII and helped defeat the Nazis. He was able to move armies faster than had ever been done before. This made him one of the most successful combat generals in U.S. history.

He became an expert in tank warfare and was an early proponent of using tanks in battle.

He was known for his drive, will, temper, and genius as a warrior. This book is filled with stories that illustrate his guiding principles.

Lessons and Takeaways

No decision is hard to make if you have all the facts.

Never take counsel of your fears.

Always do everything you ask of the men you command.

Say what you mean and mean what you say.

Anyone who thinks he's indispensable isn't.

*"A good plan, violently executed now,
is better than a perfect plan next week."*

George Patton

Select leaders for accomplishment, not for affection.

Get in shape. There is no power in a bushel of blubber.

If everyone is thinking alike, no one is thinking.

Never let the enemy pick the battle site.

Never fight a battle if nothing is to be gained by winning.

Success is how high you bounce after you hit bottom.

Better to fight for something in life than to die for nothing.

Lincoln Speaks to Leaders

by Pat Williams

Abraham Lincoln is one of America's most admired presidents. He saved the Union and helped free the slaves.

20 Powerful Lessons for Today's Leaders from America's 16th President

LINCOLN SPEAKS TO LEADERS

By GENE GRIESSMAN and PAT WILLIAMS with PEGGY MATTHEWS ROSE

Lincoln faced many struggles and overcame many obstacles in his life. Persisting through the obstacles strengthened him and prepared him for what he would face in leading the Union during the Civil War.

After the Civil War, he favored a policy of reunification with minimum retribution.

This book teaches the principles Lincoln followed to become a great leader.

Lessons and Takeaways

Challenge yourself to read at least one history book or biography a month.

Everyone in your life is there for a reason—to help shape you into a better leader or person.

Look for ways to benefit from bad times or bad experiences.

Be a possibility thinker. Think about how you can achieve your goals. If you are determined, you will find a way.

"Character is like a tree and reputation like a shadow. The shadow is what we think of it; the tree is the real thing."

Abraham Lincoln

Let your actions reflect what you believe. Walk your talk. Stand up for what you really believe in.

Success begins with willpower. Resolve to do your best.

Look for something you can improve in yourself every day.

Don't let fear hold you back. Face your fears.

21

Reagan on Leadership

by James Strock

Ronald Reagan served as president from 1981 to 1989. He was raised in a small town in Illinois, was a radio announcer, an actor, the president of the Actors Guild, then governor of California.

Reagan believed in having a smaller government and lower taxes. He increased defense spending, negotiated a nuclear arms agreement with the Soviets, and helped bring a quicker end to the Cold War.

This book teaches the things he did to be a great leader.

Lessons and Takeaways

"Surround yourself with the best people you can find, delegate authority, and don't interfere as long as the policy you've decided upon is being carried out."

"The greatest leader is not necessarily the one who does the greatest things. He is the one that gets the people to do the greatest things."

"There are no easy answers but there are simple answers. We must have the courage to do what we know is morally right."

"To grasp and hold a vision, that is the very essence of successful leadership."

Ronald Reagan

"Heroes are not braver than anyone else. They're just braver five minutes longer."

"There is no limit to the amount of good you can do if you don't care who gets the credit."

"Freedom is never more than one generation away from extinction. It must be fought for, protected, and handed on for them to do the same."

"The struggle now going on for the world will never be decided by bombs or rockets, by armies or military might. The real crisis we face today is a spiritual one; at root, it is a test of moral will and faith."

"Government is like a baby. An alimentary canal with a big appetite at one end and no responsibility at the other."

"You and I have a rendezvous with destiny. We'll preserve for our children this, the last best hope of man on Earth, or we'll sentence them to take the last step into a thousand years of darkness."

Ronald Reagan

The Founding Fathers on Leadership

by Donald Phillips

The founding fathers, George Washington, Thomas Jefferson, John Adams, Benjamin Franklin, Alexander Hamilton, John Jay and James Madison were outgunned and outmanned by England.

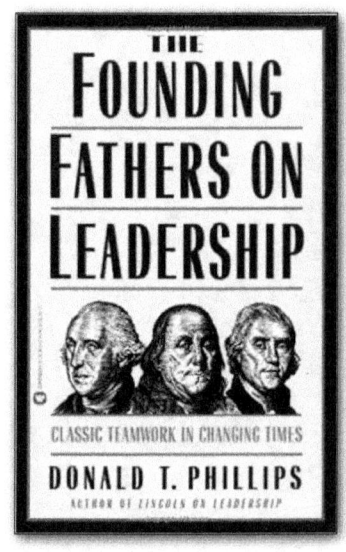

Through their passion, determination and resourcefulness, they were able to achieve the impossible.

This book explains the leadership principles they followed, how they rallied people to their cause, how they turned defeat into victory, and how they developed future leaders to govern the new nation.

Lessons and Takeaways

You should work for the future rather than only for the present moment.

Success does not only belong to the strong, but to the vigilant, the active and the brave.

Hope for the best but prepare for the worst.

Make your vision simple so that people can understand it.

Invite people to participate in your vision.

"If you want something you've never had, you must be willing to do something you've never done."

Thomas Jefferson

Consult with your advisers before every major decision.

Elevate your cause to a level that will inspire others.

Communicate with simplicity, consistency, and clarity.

Never lose sight of your vision. Take consistent action to achieve your goal.

The greater the risk, the greater the glory.

Vince Lombardi
on Leadership
by Pat Williams

Vince Lombardi was an American football player and a famous coach who became a symbol of single-minded determination to win.

Lombardi was a bold, decisive, and influential leader. He led the Green Bay Packers to six divisional titles, five national football league championships, and two super bowl wins.

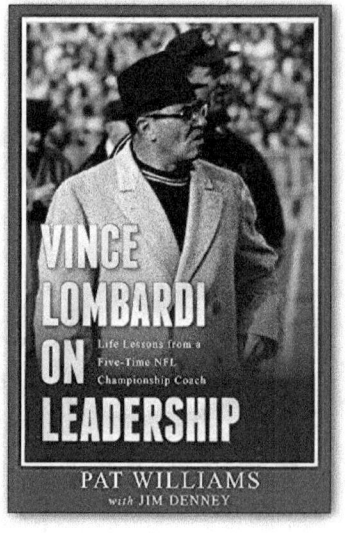

His philosophy about how to live life struck a chord with the American public. The Super Bowl trophy bears Vince Lombardi's name.

Lessons and Takeaways

"Leaders aren't born; they are made. And they are made just like anything else, through hard work."

"Success demands singleness of purpose."

"Winning is a habit. Your thoughts become your beliefs. Your beliefs become your words. Your words become your actions. Your actions become your habits. Your habits become your character."

"If you'll not settle for anything less than your best, you will be amazed at what you can accomplish in your lives."

Vince Lombardi

"The objective is to win—fairly, squarely, decently. Win by the rules, but still, win."

"Everyone has the will to win but very few have the will to prepare to win."

"Fatigue makes cowards of us all."

"Perfection is not attainable, but if we chase perfection we can catch excellence."

"There's only one way to succeed at anything, and that's to give everything."

"The greatest accomplishment is not in never falling, but in rising again after you fall."

"The harder you work, the harder it is to surrender."

*"Practice doesn't make perfect.
Perfect practice makes perfect."*

Vince Lombardi

"The difference between a successful person and others is not a lack of strength, not a lack of knowledge, but rather a lack of will."

"The price of success is hard work, dedication, and the determination that whether we win or lose, we have applied the best of ourselves to the task at hand."

"The good Lord gave you a body
that can stand most anything.
It's your mind you have to convince."

Vince Lombardi

How to Be Like Coach Wooden

by Pat Williams

John Wooden is considered the greatest NCAA basketball coach of all time. Coach Wooden led the UCLA Bruins basketball team to eighty-eight victories in a row and ten national championships.

He created the Pyramid of Success and wrote several books to share his philosophy.

In this biography, Pat Williams tells Wooden's story, then pulls out the lessons we can learn about leadership from Wooden's life.

Lessons and Takeaways

"Things turn out best for the people who make the best of the way things turn out."

"Do not let what you cannot do interfere with what you can do."

"You can't let praise or criticism get to you. It's a weakness to get caught up in either one."

"Success comes from knowing that you did your best to become the best that you are capable of becoming."

John Wooden

"If you don't have time to do it right, when will you have time to do it over?"

"If you are afraid to fail, you will never do the things you are capable of doing."

"Nothing will work unless you do."

"The true test of a man's character is what he does when no one is watching."

"Don't let yesterday take up too much of today."

Developing the Leader Within You
by John Maxwell

John Maxwell is a leadership expert. In this book, he shows the differences between various leadership styles and explains how to inspire, motivate, and influence people depending on your leadership style.

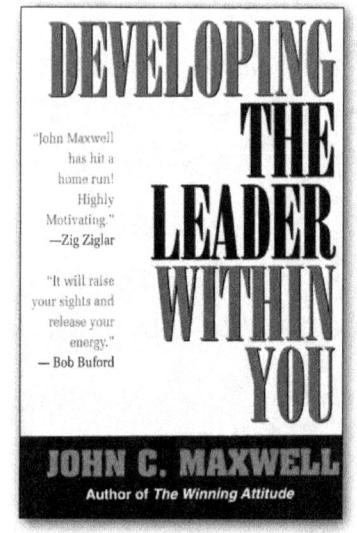

Maxwell talks about the five levels of leadership, how your character influences your leadership, how to be a better servant-leader and how to cast a vision people are more likely to embrace.

Lessons and Takeaways

Leadership is influencing and inspiring people to do better work. It involves casting a vision and motivating people to pursue it.

Leadership is the ability to obtain followers.

There are different types of leadership. The lowest level is positional leadership. That means people follow you because of your title; they have to follow you or else.

True leadership means people follow you because they want to.

Integrity is a must for a leader because what people hear, they understand. What they see, they believe.

If people understand you, you'll get their attention. If people trust you, you'll get their action.

Leaders must live by higher standards than their followers.

You can judge leaders by the size of the problems they tackle.

People buy into the leader first, then into the vision.

Leaders who gather followers add to what they can accomplish. Leaders who develop other leaders multiply their ability.

Leadership and Self Deception

by The Arbinger Institute

Leadership and Self-Deception is a parable book about a man facing challenges at work and home.

The story shows different ways that people sabotage their efforts to reach their goals.

People trap themselves in a "box" of self-justification. Then the book shows how to get out of the box by taking action right away whenever we feel we should do what's right.

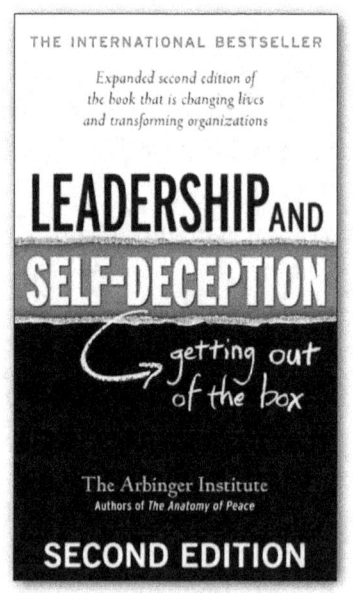

Lessons and Takeaways

An act contrary to what you feel you should do for another is called an act of "self-betrayal."

When you betray yourself, you begin to see the world in a way that justifies your self-betrayal. When you see the world in a self-justifying way, your view of reality becomes distorted.

Don't try to be perfect; try to be better.

"No matter what you're doing on the outside, people primarily respond to how you feel about them on the inside."

The Arbinger Institute

When you are feeling bothered about others, ask yourself: am I holding myself to the same standard I am demanding of them?

No conflict can be solved so long as all parties are convinced they are right. Solution is possible only when at least one party begins to consider how he might be wrong.

Leading Leaders

by Mickey Addison

Colonel Mickey Addison shares the leadership principles he learned in sports, in the Boy Scouts, and in his 30-year career in the U.S. Air Force.

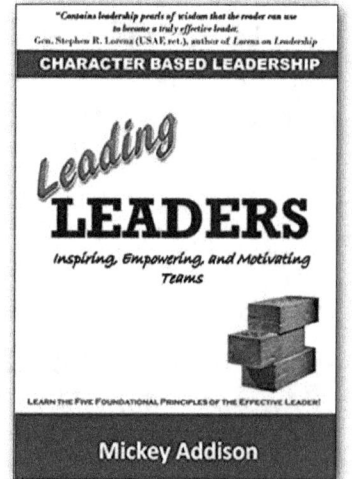

He uses personal stories and anecdotes to illustrate the principles of character-based leadership.

This book is a must-read for anyone who wants to become a better leader by improving their character.

Lessons and Takeaways

Leadership is getting people to do what they don't want to so that they can achieve what they want to achieve.

The foundation of successful leaders, the key to their effectiveness, is their character. Without character, no leader can be successful for long.

Leaders must model respect and demand it of their teams. Respect is earned by the way you do your job, how you treat others, and how you carry yourself. Make your expectations known and reinforce those expectations often.

"Leaders have integrity. The measure of a person's integrity is how willing they are to do the right thing, even when no one is watching."

Mickey Addison

Leaders take charge and make sure their teams understand what they need to be doing and why.

Leaders invest themselves in their team's success. When someone fails, they usually fail for one of three reasons: they weren't trained, they weren't given proper resources, or they weren't led.

Leaders set high standards. Little things add up to big things. A leader who's engaged and pays attention to the little things creates a culture where the team pays attention to the little things.

"The leader encourages teamwork because every organization functions as a team. Everyone needs each other to be successful. The team wins or loses together. No excuses."

Mickey Addison

Next Generation Leader

by Andy Stanley

Pastor Andy Stanley has been training young Christian leaders to learn, grow and lead for over 20 years.

In this book, he talks about five characteristics that determine how strong a leader you can become: courage, clarity, competence, coachability and character.

He shows how to discover and play from your strengths, how to harness your fears, how to leverage uncertainty, and how to find and follow a leadership coach so that you can develop into a stronger leader.

Lessons and Takeaways

Don't strive to be a well-rounded leader. Instead, discover your zone and stay there, then delegate everything else.

Admitting a weakness is a sign of strength. Acknowledging weakness doesn't make a leader less effective.

Leadership is about moving boldly into the future in spite of uncertainty and risk.

"Leaders are not always the first
to see the need for change,
but they are the first to act."

Andy Stanley

Everybody in your organization benefits when you delegate responsibilities that fall outside your core competency. Thoughtful delegation will allow someone else in your organization to shine. Your weakness is someone's opportunity.

The first person to step out in a new direction is viewed as the leader. And being the first to step out requires courage. In this way, courage establishes leadership.

The 4 Dimensions of Extraordinary Leadership

by Jenni Catron

Jenni Catron is an executive church leader. In this book, she shows how everyone has the capacity to become a better leader.

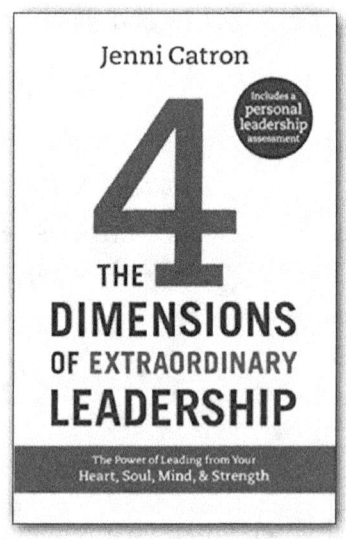

She talks about leadership principles found in the Great Commandment: "Love the Lord your God with all your heart and with all your soul and with all your mind and with all your strength."

She talks about how you can become a better leader by developing your heart, soul, mind, and strength.

Lessons and Takeaways

Filter every decision you make in leadership through the lens of what is God-honoring.

The heart of a leader is the truest part of who they are. Your heart is what connects you with others the most.

Lead yourself well to lead others better.

Great leaders develop other leaders.

Actions speak louder than intentions. Our leadership will be evaluated by what we do, not what we intend.

Leaders offer hope in the midst of intense circumstances.

Leadership involves heartaches, disappointments and mistakes. It means relentless growth and frequent failure.

Leaders aren't leading for themselves; they are leading for others.

Leadership is only as strong as the leader. Your leadership journey must begin with leading yourself well.

Leaders live in a constant state of tension. We live between what is and what could be.

The Heart of Leadership

by Mark Miller

What sets great leaders apart from all the rest? Is it people skills, execution skills, the ability to paint a vision? Yes, but that's just the tip of the iceberg.

What's the key? It's their leadership character.

In this entertaining business fable, Mark Miller, the VP of Leadership of Chick-fil-A, shares the five character traits of the world's top leaders and how to develop them.

Leadership skills are easy to learn, but they won't take you far. Surprisingly, leadership is all about your heart.

Lessons and Takeaways

You can lead with or without a title. If you wait until you get a title, you may wait forever.

When you expect the best from people, you will often see more in them than they see in themselves.

When faced with a challenging or difficult situation, the best leaders most often respond with courage; less mature leaders, or non-leaders often choose another path—one with less risk, conflict, and personal discomfort.

"If your heart is not right, no one cares about your leadership skills."

Mark Miller

Leaders are dealers in hope.

The best leaders don't blame others; they own their actions and their outcomes.

The Servant

by James Hunter

In this business parable, James Hunter teaches the foundational principles of servant leadership through the story of a man whose life is out of control. He attends a leadership retreat and learns the keys to leadership from a monk.

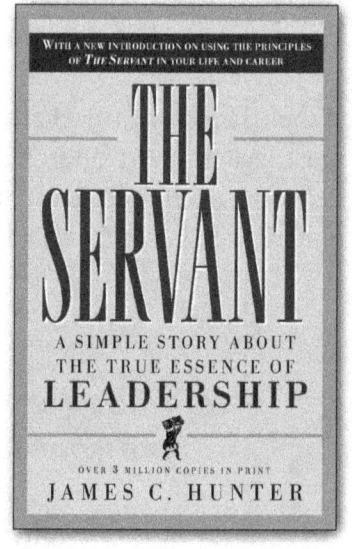

He learns that the key to leadership is not power but trust, which comes from service, love, relationships, and sacrifice.

Leadership isn't about talent or skills; leadership begins with developing respect and caring for the people around you.

This book will teach you how to become a better leader as you enjoy a wonderful story.

Lessons and Takeaways

Great leaders have these qualities: humility, respect, self-control, honesty, commitment, determination, gratitude, and communication skills.

The key then to leadership is accomplishing the tasks at hand while building relationships.

As leaders we do not create growth. The best we can do is create an environment that is conducive to growth. It is like planting a garden. You do not cause the seeds to grow. To grow is their natural purpose in life.

"What we think or what we believe is of little consequence in the end. The only thing of consequence is what we do."

James Hunter

We should be kind to others. How far you go in life depends on being tender with the young, compassionate with the aged, sympathetic with the striving, and tolerant of the weak and strong. Because someday in life, you will have been all of these.

The Tiny Warrior

by D.J. Vanas

D.J. Vanas shares wisdom from his Odawa American Indian background and his experience as an officer in the U.S. Air Force.

This is a wonderful parable about a young man learning success principles from his elder.

The Tiny Warrior teaches how to look inside to discover your strengths and power—your inner warrior—so that you can realize your goals and serve the people around you.

Lessons and Takeaways

The child you were will always affect and be a part of who you are.

You can't outrun your life's problems when those problems are within.

A river's water flows over rocks. Whether you go over, under, around or through, find a way to reach your goals.

"Settling for second best or good enough is neither the best nor enough for your life."

D.J Vanas

You will feel true joy when you align your talent and ability with your life path.

Mistakes happen. Forgive yourself, learn the lessons, and move on.

Once you know your purpose and pursue it, life changes from a frustrating struggle to an adventure.

Knowing what you want to do with your life is much more important than how you will get there.

Don't mistake contentment and security for true happiness.

Don't let your wants keep you from getting your needs in life.

Today's choices determine where you'll be tomorrow.

The sooner you stop making excuses, the sooner you'll begin to make true progress toward your dreams.

"You will be rewarded and judged by your actions, not your intentions."

D.J. Vanas

They Call Me Coach

by John Wooden

Legendary basketball coach John Wooden shares stories about his life, his players and the principles he followed on the way to winning 10 NCAA championships.

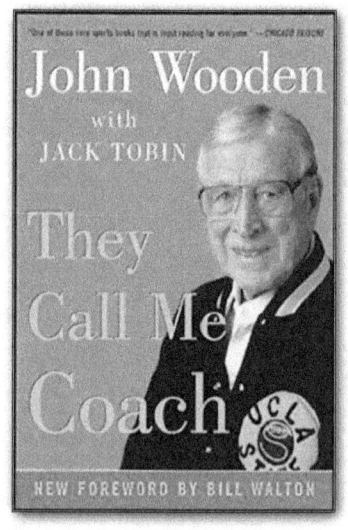

Wooden was a big believer in hard work, preparedness, and mastering the fundamentals. He believed that if you did those things, the results would take care of themselves.

This is not just a basketball book; it's a book filled with success principles anyone can use to create a great life.

Lessons and Takeaways

"Ninety percent of the time, the game is going to be decided in the final five minutes. When two teams are evenly matched, the better-conditioned team will usually execute better when fatigue sets in, and will probably win."

"Be more concerned with your character than your reputation because your character is what you really are, while your reputation is merely what others think you are."

John Wooden

"Have the patience to always follow your game plan."

"Talent is God-given. Be humble. Fame is man-given. Be grateful. Conceit is self-given. Be careful."

"Never mistake activity for achievement."

John Wooden

Part Three

Teamwork

The Four Commitments
of a Winning Team
by Mark Eaton

Mark Eaton was a starting center for the Utah Jazz for ten years. Incredibly, he didn't begin playing basketball until he was 21 years old. Wilt Chamberlain told Mark that if he focused on his strength—playing defense—he could become a great player.

Mark became a role player for his team and went on to become a record-breaking Hall of Fame player.

This book shows how, by focusing on your strengths and becoming a role player, you can be your best as you help your team shine.

Lessons and Takeaways

Unselfishness is the most important team attitude.

If you give 100% all of the time, somehow, things will work out in the end.

"The best way to help your team is to know your job, do what you're asked to do, make your teammates look good, and protect your teammates."

Mark Eaton

"I'll do whatever it takes to win games, whether it's sitting on a bench waving a towel, handing a cup of water to a teammate, or hitting the game-winning shot."

Kobe Bryant

2 Hour House

by Brian Conaway

A group of Texas homebuilders wanted to set a new world record for building a 2000-square-foot house from the ground up. The house needed to pass a building inspection to qualify.

To do so, they would have to pour a concrete slab that hardened in only 22 minutes and paint the house in five minutes.

It took two years of planning and over 1000 volunteers to pull it off.

This book shares the things they learned about leadership and teamwork along the way.

Lessons and Takeaways

Your goal should never change. You may have to try different approaches, but the goal needs to say the same.

Asking "what if?" questions gets creativity going. What if we did it this way? What if we tried it that way? No idea is too ridiculous. Sometimes, an approach that seems ridiculous ends up being the best one. Experiment with different approaches.

"There's no substitute for practice and planning if you want to see your dream become a reality."

Brian Conaway

Don't be shy about asking experts for their advice; their experience can save you a lot of time.

When you know and commit to your values, decision-making becomes a lot easier.

If your desire is strong enough and your plans are flexible enough, you can accomplish anything you set your mind to.

The Five Dysfunctions of a Team

by Patrick Lencioni

In this leadership fable, Patrick Lencioni focuses on pitfalls that can hurt a team's performance.

The CEO of a company is trying to unite a team that isn't producing and that's threatening to bring down the whole company.

Throughout the story, the CEO learns five reasons why the team is struggling and is able to come up with simple solutions that help turn the team around and save the company.

Lessons and Takeaways

Great teams do not hold back with one another. They are unafraid to air their dirty laundry. They admit their mistakes, weaknesses, and concerns without fear of reprisal.

When people don't unload their opinions and feel like they've been listened to, they won't really get on board with the leaders' decisions.

"Politics is when people choose their words and actions based on how they want others to react rather than based on what they really think."

Patrick Lencioni

If you don't trust each other, then you won't engage in open, constructive, ideological conflict—and you'll continue to preserve a sense of artificial harmony.

Great teams make clear and timely decisions and move forward with complete buy-in from every team member, even those who voted against the decision. They leave meetings confident that no one on the team is quietly harboring doubts about whether to support the actions agreed on.

Part Four

Success Principles

A Game Plan for Life

by John Wooden

Of all the books he wrote, this was John Wooden's favorite because it's about the power of mentorship.

The first half of the book focuses on the people who helped Wooden develop his values: Wooden's mentors, including his college coach, Abraham Lincoln and Mother Teresa.

The second half is about people Coach Wooden mentored: Kareem Abdul-Jabbar, Bill Walton, and his other players.

This book is all about how to achieve success without sacrificing your principles.

Lessons and Takeaways

You need mentors if you want to succeed. A good mentor should have already done what you want to do. They should fit into your learning style so that it's easier for you to learn from them.

You must be willing to do the things the mentor says you need to do, not just the things that are comfortable. Breaking out of your comfort zone will help you achieve things you didn't think were possible.

You'll learn key things from being a mentor to others— things like respect for yourself and your mentee, the power of influence, and even humility.

John Wooden's father gave him a card with seven rules for living: be true to yourself, make each day your masterpiece, help others, drink deeply from good books, make friendship a fine art, build a shelter for a rainy day, pray for guidance, and give thanks for your blessings every day.

Don't whine, complain, or make excuses; just do the best you can. Nobody can do more than that.

Nobody is bigger than their team.

A Message to Millennials
by Charlie and Tracey Jones

This leadership book is filled with tips that will help anyone become a more productive, valuable, and promotable person at work.

Every employer looks for people who are teachable, accountable, purposeful, trustworthy, respectable, and promotable. They look for goal-oriented self-starters they don't have to babysit.

A Message to Millennials shows you how you can be all of those things so that you can be happy and successful in your work life.

Lessons and Takeaways

Many people don't actually dislike their jobs; they just complain for the sake of complaining. By focusing on what they don't like about their jobs, before long, they talk themselves into hating their job. Approach your job with a good attitude, and eventually, you'll start enjoying it. What you think about your job will determine how well you do.

Before you can lead, you need to learn how to follow.

Anyone can find a problem. The thing that will make you stand out is finding the solution.

"Life isn't about doing what you like to do. Life is about doing what you ought to do."

Charlie "Tremendous" Jones

Stay away from the water cooler at work to limit your exposure to gossip and negativity.

Effective followers seize every opportunity to be a part of something greater than themselves.

If you're not pulling your share of the load, someone in your team has to pick up the slack.

Iron is sharpened and diamonds are cut in the fire of pressure and challenges. Adversity creates character.

Learn from your mistakes so that they become stepping stones to progress.

Growth only happens outside your comfort zone, so be willing to take leaps of faith. If you do what you fear, the fear will disappear.

If you don't know what to do next, just do something. A ship can only change course when it's in motion.

"Your dream job will call your non-dream job for references."

Tracey Jones

A Survival Guide for Life

by Bear Grylls

Bear Grylls is a world-famous adventurer who's been to the wildest places on Earth. In this book, he shares the lessons he learned from his adventures.

He talks about planning and executing goals, facing danger, pushing yourself even when you're ready to quit, and how to sharpen your instincts.

The tips in this book will help you achieve your goals faster as you live a purpose-driven meaningful life.

Lessons and Takeaways

Little faith is involved in setting out on a journey where the destination is certain and every step in between has been mapped in detail. Bravery and trust are about leaving camp in the dark when we do not know the route ahead and cannot be certain we will ever return.

> *"Life rewards the dogged,*
> *not the qualified."*

Bear Grylls

This is your life; be bold with it. Live it with energy and purpose in the direction that excites you. Listen to your heart and look for your dreams; they are God-inspired.

You are wonderfully and powerfully made. In other words; it is no accident you are good at certain things!

An easy life is a boring and uneventful life; the storms in life will make you stronger and will prepare you for bigger storms that will come later in life. A hard life is better than an easy life.

The journey is often just as much fun and just as exciting as reaching the goal itself.

Dare to Succeed

by Mark Burnett

Before creating and producing, *Survivor* and *Shark Tank* TV series, Mark Burnett was selling t-shirts on a beach in California. This is the story of how he transformed his life.

Burnett had been a British military paratrooper and an open-water SCUBA diver before moving to the U.S. Frustrated with his aimless life on the beach, he decided to use what he learned in the military to achieve more.

This book shows how to realize your dreams by facing your fears, becoming determined, and being willing to do things most people are not willing to do.

Lessons and Takeaways

Facing your fears robs them of their power.

There's nothing like biting off more than you can chew and then chewing anyway.

"Attitude produces character, and character produces hope."

Mark Burnett

The day you step outside your comfort zone by making success your goal is the day you discover that adversity, risk, and daring will make life sweeter than you ever imagined.

The best person to get something done is a busy person.

Americans are into results. Americans don't care where you came from, what your family did, what school you graduated from; they care about if you can deliver the results. That's what makes America great.

Courage isn't the absence of fear, it's acting in spite of your fear.

Do Hard Things

by Alex and Brett Harris

Until about 100 years ago, once you turned 14 years old, you began to share your family's responsibilities and work as an adult. You were expected to behave like an adult.

This book encourages teens to take responsibility and work hard so that their teen years can be a launching pad for a great life.

By getting a job, setting ambitious goals, and having good grades in school, teens can lay the foundation for a great life.

Lessons and Takeaways

All effort—even failed effort—produces muscle.

The teen years are the training ground for future leaders who dare to be responsible.

*"Never trying is a lot worse
than trying and losing."*

Alex & Brett Harris

Don't let anyone look down on you because you are young, but set an example for the believers in speech, life, love, faith and purity.

*"Great faith is the product of great fights.
Great testimonies are the outcome
of great tests. Great triumphs can
only come out of great trials."*

Alex & Brett Harris

Don't Eat the Marshmallow Yet!

by Joachim de Posada

Why do some people succeed and others fail?

In a famous study, young children were left in a room, each with a marshmallow.

They were given the choice of eating it right away or fifteen minutes later. The children were promised an extra marshmallow as a reward if they waited.

Some ate theirs right away. Others waited.

A decade later, researchers discovered that the children who held out for the reward became more successful adults than those who gobbled their marshmallows immediately.

In this wonderful parable, you'll see that delayed gratification pays off.

Lessons and Takeaways

Every morning in Africa, a gazelle wakes up. It knows it must run faster than the fastest lion, or it will be killed. Every morning, a lion wakes up. It knows it must outrun the slowest gazelle, or it will starve to death. It doesn't matter whether you are a lion or a gazelle; when the sun comes up, you'd better be running!

Successful people are willing to do things that unsuccessful people are not willing to do.

Knowledge isn't power; applied knowledge is power. If you know and you don't do something, you don't know.

Purpose + Passion + Action = Peace of Mind

"Success doesn't depend on
your past or current circumstances.
Success depends on your willingness
to do what's required to become successful.
The day you act on that willingness
is your first step toward success."

Joachim de Posada

Eat that Frog

by Brian Tracy

There's an old saying that if the first thing you do each morning is eat a live frog, you'll know that you're done with the worst thing you'll have to do all day. It's downhill from there.

Since there isn't time to do everything on your to-do list, successful people know they need to do the most important tasks first. They tackle their most challenging tasks first. They eat their frogs.

This book is filled with tips to help you get the most important things done so that you can reach your goals faster.

Lessons and Takeaways

The 80/20 rule says that 80% of your success will come from 20% of the things you do. That's why you need to determine what needs to be done first and what can wait for later.

Decide exactly what you want. Write it down. Set a deadline. Make a list of everything you can think of that you're going to have to do to achieve your goal. Organize the list into a plan. Take action immediately. Resolve to do something every day that moves you toward your goal.

Plan your days. Every minute spent planning saves 10 minutes in execution. Proper planning prevents poor performance.

List all your major goals, projects, and tasks by priority and work on the most important task first because there will never be enough time to do everything you have to do.

What one skill, if you developed and did it in an excellent fashion, would have the greatest positive impact on your life? Focus on learning that skill.

Seek the lesson in every setback or difficulty.

Look for the good in every situation.

Look for the solution to every problem.

Think and talk continually about your goals.

Flight Plan

by Brian Tracy

Just like a pilot needs to plan their flights by making a flight plan, we need to plan our life and goals by doing the same. Everyone needs to have clear goals, plans, and schedules to get them where they want to be—a plan that will guide you on your journey.

After planning, you need the courage to take action; to faithfully step out with no guarantees of success.

Then you must be prepared to make course adjustments and resolve in advance that you will keep going until you reach your destination. This book teaches the steps to success.

Lessons and Takeaways

The most important part of achieving any goal isn't the goal itself, it's the person you have to become to reach that goal.

Decide upon your destination. Decide exactly what you want, write it down, and make a plan to achieve it.

Take off on your journey. Take action. Launch toward your goal. Step out on faith. Take the first step with no guarantee of success.

Make course corrections. Expect problems, difficulties, and challenges. Hope for the best but prepare for the worst. Respond to your challenges effectively until you achieve your goal.

Every problem you've experienced has been sent to you at the exact time, teaching you something you need to know to be more successful and happier in the future.

Start believing that everything that happens to you will eventually help you reach your goal.

Believe that you are destined to be a great success in life. Then take massive action to achieve your goal.

Passion for Possibility

by Jose Feliciano

Jose Feliciano's parents were both deaf. They taught Jose that the place of your biggest challenge is the source of your biggest strength, so don't focus on your limitations but on your possibilities.

By focusing on being the best version of yourself, you can achieve great things and live a wonderful life.

This book is filled with tools that will help you become your best.

Lessons and Takeaways

Spectators look and act differently than those in the race. The racers have a purpose and a goal.

Doubt is the father of all negative emotions and the thief that steals our dreams and makes us play it safe.

Inactivity is a conscious decision not to move forward in our lives.

When your visions are clear, decision-making becomes easy.

"The finish line represents more
than the end of a long race.
It's a celebration of the hundreds
of hours you spent training and
preparing before race day, fulfilling
a long-range plan to succeed."

Jose Feliciano

Keys to Positive Thinking

by Napoleon Hill

Napoleon Hill is the author of *Think and Grow Rich* and *Keys to Success*. This book is a compilation of Napoleon Hill's teachings and wisdom.

It's a step-by-step plan to help you develop a positive mental attitude. Your attitude determines your altitude. You need to learn how to protect it because as soon as your attitude diminishes, so do your results.

This book includes quick daily exercises to help you maintain a positive mental attitude.

Lessons and Takeaways

"The starting point of all achievement is desire. Weak desire produces weak results."

"Whatever the mind can conceive and believe, it can achieve."

"You are the master of your destiny. You can influence, direct, and control your own environment. You can make your life what you want it to be."

"Every adversity, failure,
and heartache carries with it
the seed of an equal or greater benefit."

Napoleon Hill

If you can't do great things, do small things in a great way.

Do not wait: the time will never be just right. Start where you stand, and work whatever tools you may have at your command and better tools will be found as you go along.

Set your mind on a definite goal and observe how quickly the world stands aside to let you pass.

Million Dollar Habits

by Brian Tracy

Most of the things you think and do are determined by your habits. You can change your habits, replacing ineffective ones with habits that help you achieve your goals.

In this book, you'll learn how to develop the habits successful people use so that you can be more successful in whatever you do.

This book will help you make better decisions, think more effectively, and get the results you want.

Lessons and Takeaways

Your life is the sum of your choices, decisions, and actions. You can change your future by changing your behaviors. When it comes down to it, your habits determine your future.

Successful people expect to be successful. Happy people expect to be happy. Popular people expect to be liked by other people. Develop the habit of happy expectations.

You become what you think about most of the time because what you think about becomes your self-image. By thinking about what you want to achieve, you change your self-image. Once you believe it's possible, you start taking action.

Becoming a continuous learner will help you become a top performer in your field.

Winners set goals and take initiative. They don't wait for things to get better; they do something to make things better.

Perseverance is one of the most important habits you can develop. The ability to come back from behind puts you ahead of 90% of the population.

Your people skills determine how high you will go because you can accomplish much more through other people than by yourself.

Poor, Smart, Rich

by John Segal

John Segal was a successful businessman. For 19 years, he taught Sunday school classes for middle and high school students.

When he asked his students what they wanted to learn, they said they wanted to learn practical things about real life —how to earn a living, get a good job and how to get rich.

This book is based on what John taught in his classes. The classes were built around six simple and powerful rules that are basic to good living.

Lessons and Takeaways

People who succeed in life do things in a special order. They get an education, a good job, find a good partner to marry, have children, and move to safe neighborhoods with good schools. If you do things in this order, your chances of success are 80% or more.

People who fail in life do things in the wrong order: boy meets girl, they have sex, girl gets pregnant and drops out of school, girl gets on welfare, boy leaves, girl lives with relatives, girl meets new guy, they don't get married so girl can keep welfare, more kids, more guys, lives in a rough neighborhood with bad schools and crime. If you do things in this order, your chances of success are 20% or less because you're stuck.

The first three rules are minimum goals to keep you out of poverty:

1 - Don't get pregnant or get someone pregnant before high school graduation and marriage.

2 - Get a job and build on it.

3 - Get married and stay married.

The three higher goals will help you make the leap into middle class and beyond:

1 - Work hard on your job but work harder on improving yourself.

2 - Write down your life goals and focus on achieving them.

3 - Seek a positive, powerful relationship with God.

Rhinoceros Success

by Scott Alexander

Imagine if you woke up tomorrow morning as a full-grown rhinoceros and lived your life as a rhino does.

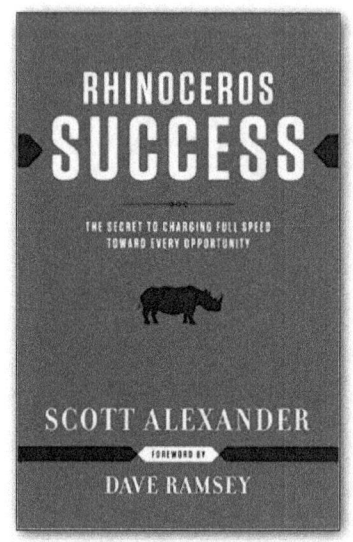

You'd charge your way to success. You would audaciously pursue your goals. You'd make your life an exciting adventure. Your thick skin would help you be tenacious and persistent. You'd achieve more than you ever had before.

This fun book is all about developing a winning attitude, taking action, and reaching your goals.

Lessons and Takeaways

Rhinos don't hesitate or stop; they always take massive action. They keep their momentum by charging all the time.

Associate with other rhinos. Your friends need to be positive, encouraging go-getters like you. You become like the people you associate with.

Rhinos don't sit and mope about how hard their goals are. They are optimistic. Their optimism helps them charge and find opportunities in their challenges.

"When you get mad, harness your energy and use it to charge after your goal."

Scott Alexander

Develop a thick skin to withstand criticism from naysayers.

Charge with singleness of purpose. Stay focused on your goal.

Rich Dad Poor Dad
by Robert Kiyosaki

This is Robert Kiyosaki's story of growing up with two dads—his real father and the father of his best friend, his rich dad—and how both men shaped his thoughts about money and investing.

Kiyosaki shows how you don't need to earn a high income to become rich. He explains why your house is not an asset. He warns not to expect the school system to teach kids about money. He also explains the difference between an asset and a liability.

It's a book that will change the way you think about money.

Lessons and Takeaways

In school, you learn that mistakes are bad, and you're punished for making them. But people were created to learn by making mistakes. You learn to walk by falling down. If you never fell down, you'd never learn how to walk.

If you're the kind of person with no guts, you give up every time life pushes you. If you're that kind of person, you'll live all your life playing it safe, doing the right things, and saving yourself for something that never happens. Then, you die a boring old man.

"Winners are not afraid of losing, but losers are. Failure is part of the process of success. People who avoid failure also avoid success."

Robert Kiyosaki

The single most powerful asset we all have is our mind. If it is trained well, it can create enormous wealth in what seems to be an instant.

If you realize that you're the problem, then you can change yourself, learn something, and grow wiser. Don't blame other people for your problems.

We all have tremendous potential, and we are all blessed with gifts. Yet, the one thing that holds all of us back is some degree of self-doubt. It is not so much the lack of technical information that holds us back, but more the lack of self-confidence.

In the real world, something more than just grades is required to win. You need something called guts, chutzpah, audacity, daring, and tenacity. This decides your future much more than school grades.

"There's a difference between being poor and being broke. Broke is temporary. Poor is eternal."

Robert Kiyosaki

The Difference Maker

by John Maxwell

How come two people with the same skills and abilities and in the same situation get completely different results? The difference is their attitude. Your attitude determines how you see everything and, ultimately, how you perform.

It's not just about what you do, but how you do it. A positive attitude helps you do everything better.

Having a positive attitude doesn't guarantee success, but you'll always be more successful with a positive attitude. This book shows why.

Lessons and Takeaways

Attitude is an inward feeling expressed by outward behavior. You will always project on the outside what you feel on the inside.

Your attitude colors every aspect of your life. It is like the mind's paintbrush.

Your attitude makes a difference in how you face challenges and deal with people.

When you are discouraged, give yourself a pep talk; "This, too, shall pass. Things could be worse. I can do it. I'm a winner. Every day in every way, I'm getting better and better, stronger and stronger, smarter and smarter."

Your perspective on the problem, not the problem itself, usually determines your success or failure.

Sooner or later, we all get what we expect. So expect the best.

It may not be your fault for being down, but it's your fault for not getting yourself back up.

Sometimes you win, and sometimes you learn.

Judge your day by the seeds sown, not by the harvest reaped.

The emotion you continually feed is the one that will dominate your life.

The Go-Giver

by Bob Burg

This is the story of a young man named Joe. Joe's a go-getter. He yearns for success but feels that the harder and faster he works, the further his goals seem to be.

Joe seeks advice from a series of successful "go-givers": a restaurant owner, a CEO, a financial adviser, a businessman, and a real estate broker.

They each teach him how he can be more successful by using the power of giving.

Lessons and Takeaways

Your influence is determined by how well you place other people's needs ahead of yours.

Your income is determined by how many people you serve and how well you serve them.

The most valuable gift you have to offer is yourself, so be authentic.

The key to effective giving is to stay open to receiving. It's like breathing. You breathe in, and you breathe out. Both work together.

*"A person's value is measured
by how many people he influences,
how many lives he touches,
and how much he gives,
not by how much he receives."*

Bob Burg

The Little Red Book
of Wisdom
by Mark DeMoss

Mark DeMoss owns a prominent publicity agency and wrote this book to share what he learned in many years of business.

His book is filled with tips and lessons that will help anyone simplify their life and focus more on the things that are truly important.

DeMoss talks about the importance of listening and thinking instead of talking and doing, shows the power of writing a letter, the value of eating lunch alone, and the wisest decision anyone can make.

A wonderful book filled with timeless truths.

Lessons and Takeaways

Under promise and over-deliver.

Write letters. A letter's impact almost always exceeds the writer's effort.

Honesty can be costly, but telling the truth is always good in the long run.

Think twice before being openly critical, rude, or angry.

Great leaders are great servants first of all. Great service is modest and understated, in speech and action. Understatement is self-restraint, and self-restraint is hardly a sign of weakness. On the contrary, wisely used, few things carry more power.

"All you can do is all you can do, but all you can do is enough. We can't control the rain, but we can pull out an umbrella. We can't control a harsh word leveled at us, but we can return with a soft answer."

Mark DeMoss

The Richest Man in Babylon

by George Clason

George Clason founded a map company and published the first road atlas of the United States and Canada. In 1926, George Clason started writing the finance parables, which became *The Richest Man in Babylon*.

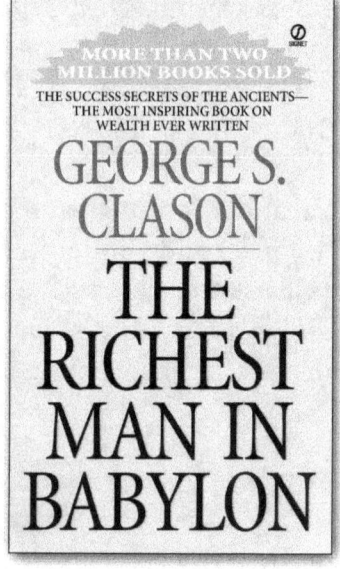

This classic book reveals the secret to personal wealth through fascinating stories that draw you right in.

It teaches some very simple things anyone can do to save money and accumulate wealth over your life. Each of his points is made through parables set in ancient Babylon.

Lessons and Takeaways

"Willpower is but the unflinching purpose to carry the task you set for yourself to fulfillment."

Where determination lies, the way can be found.

Proper preparation is the key to our success. Our acts can be no wiser than our thoughts. Our thinking can be no wiser than our understanding.

Good luck can be enticed by accepting opportunity.

Wealth, like a tree, grows from a tiny seed. The first penny you save is the seed from which your tree of wealth shall grow. The sooner you plant that seed, the sooner shall the tree grow. And the more faithfully you nourish and water that tree with consistent savings, the sooner may you bask in contentment beneath its shade.

"Opportunity is a haughty goddess who wastes no time with those who are unprepared."

George Clason

The Slight Edge
by Jeff Olson

The Slight Edge explains a way of thinking that helps you make choices that lead to success. It's about the compound effect small decisions make over time.

It shows how to create powerful results from your daily activities and helps you understand that consistent and persistent small actions will eventually produce amazing results.

This is an eye-opening book. After reading *The Slight Edge*, everything you've read in other personal development books will make a lot more sense.

Lessons and Takeaways

Successful people do what unsuccessful people are unwilling to do.

What you do every day matters. Successful people just do the things that seem to make no difference in the act of doing them, and they do them over and over until the compound effect kicks in.

The journey starts with a single step, not with thinking about taking a step.

There are two kinds of habits: those that serve you and those that don't.

Successful people take full responsibility for who they are, where they are, and everything that happens to them.

Any time you see what looks like a breakthrough, it is always the result of a long series of little things, done consistently over time.

Take care with what you think. Because what you think, multiplied by action plus time, will create what you get.

There is a natural progression to everything in life: plant, cultivate, harvest.

The Success System that Never Fails

by W. Clement Stone

W. Clement Stone's life was a rags-to-riches story. He went from selling newspapers on street corners to founding the Combined Insurance Company of America and donating hundreds of millions of dollars to charities.

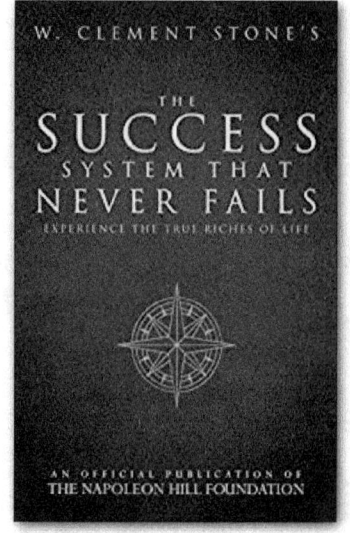

Stone co-wrote *Success Through a Positive Mental Attitude* with Napoleon Hill.

In this book, he shares the success principles he followed. He does it by sharing stories about how successful people achieved their goals.

Lessons and Takeaways

All success hinges on three things: being inspired to take action, developing the know-how needed to reach your goals, and learning from your mistakes.

Take a chance. Success is achieved by those who try. Where there is nothing to lose by trying and a great deal to gain if successful, by all means, try!

Keep your thoughts off the things you don't want by keeping them on the things you want.

Do the right things because they are right.

Do what you're afraid to do. When you let fear keep you from taking action, you pass opportunity by.

An inspired person can overcome all obstacles. If you want something, go after it. Do it now!

All personal achievement starts in the mind of the individual. If you want something badly enough, where you believe it's possible and you take action, you can achieve it.

Turn every disadvantage into an advantage. Every adversity has the seed of an equivalent or greater benefit.

You can achieve your goals if you follow success principles and take consistent and persistent action.

Who Moved My Cheese?

by Spencer Johnson

This is a story of four mice who live in a maze, looking for cheese to make them happy.

In this book, cheese is a metaphor for whatever you want in life. The maze is where you look for it.

This book helps you prepare for change and be ready to quickly adapt when change happens so that you can get your cheese more quickly.

Lessons and Takeaways

See what you're doing wrong, laugh at it, change, and do better.

People resist change, because they are afraid of it.

What do you need to let go of, and what do you need to move on to?

Change happens when the pain of holding on becomes greater than the fear of letting go.

Noticing small changes early helps you adapt to the bigger change that are to come.

Life is no straight and easy corridor along which we travel free and unhampered, but a maze of passages, through which we must seek our way, lost and confused, now and again checked in a blind alley. But always, if we have faith, a door will open for us.

"The thing you are afraid of is never as bad as what you imagine.
The fear you let build up
in your mind is worse than
the situation that actually exists."

Spencer Johnson

Winning Every Day

by Lou Holtz

Lou Holtz coached the Notre Dame Football Team to nine bowl games and a national championship.

He did it by designing a game plan for his players that helped maximize their opportunities. In this book, he shares the ten strategies you can take to achieve your goals faster.

He talks about raising your standards, being willing to sacrifice, setting goals, being flexible in your approach, and refusing to quit.

A fun book filled with stories from his football teams.

Lessons and Takeaways

The attitude you choose to have toward life will determine whether you realize your goals.

The road to success is filled with setbacks and problems you'll have to solve. If you respond to setbacks quickly and positively, you'll reach your goals faster.

Successful people stay 100% focused on their main goal.

"Take pride in making sacrifices and in having self-discipline."

Lou Holtz

Things are always changing. Take advantage of change by adapting quickly. Whoever adjusts first wins.

Dreams fuel your enthusiasm and vision. They give you a burning desire to do what it takes to win.

Commit to excellence, show care for others, and be trustworthy.

Always ask yourself, "What's the right thing to do?" then do it.

Set high standards for yourself. Do everything to the best of your ability.

The Fred Factor

by Mark Sanborn

This is the true story of Fred, a mailman who loves his job and who truly cares about the people he serves. Fred always goes the extra mile handling the mail and treats everyone as a friend.

This book teaches simple steps you can take to transform your life from ordinary to extraordinary.

You'll learn four principles: how to build strong relationships, how to make a difference, how to create value in others, and how to reinvent yourself.

Lessons and Takeaways

Everyone makes a difference, either in a positive or negative way.

Nobody can prevent you from choosing to be exceptional.

There are no unimportant jobs, just people who feel unimportant doing their jobs.

You can reinvent yourself at any time.

Success is mainly built on two things: relationships and believing that you have what it takes to reach your dreams and goals.

"A job's satisfaction level isn't determined by how hard or easy it is or if it is a high paying job; a job's satisfaction is determined by your mindset and how well you do it."

Mark Sanborn

Part Five

Free Enterprise

Beware of the
Naked Man Who
Offers You His Shirt

by Harvey Mackay

Harvey Mackay played golf in school. He became an envelope salesman, joined a golf club, and sold envelopes to the local businesspeople he met at the club. He became the number one salesperson in his company and eventually bought another envelope company. Today, his company sells over 100 million dollars of envelopes every year.

This book is filled with common-sense tips that will help you become better at whatever you do.

Lessons and Takeaways

Good habits are as addictive as bad habits and a lot more rewarding.

When you wake up every day, you have two choices: you can either be positive or negative, an optimist or a pessimist. Choose to be an optimist. It's all a matter of perspective.

One mistake will never kill you; the same mistake over and over again will.

People begin to become successful the minute they decide to be.

When someone with money meets someone with experience, the person with the experience winds up with the money, and the person with the money winds up with the experience.

"When you kill a little time,
you may be murdering opportunity."

Harvey Mackay

Eat Mor Chikin
Inspire More People
by Truett Cathy

Truett Cathy opened a small restaurant in 1946. Twenty-one years later he opened the first Chick-fil-A restaurant. The rest is history.

He achieved his success by being a servant leader and teaching his employees to be servant leaders. When a Chick-fil-A employee tells you, "My Pleasure," they're letting you know it's their pleasure to serve you, and it reminds them that it's a privilege to have the opportunity to serve someone else.

This book will challenge you to focus on other people. Success will follow.

Lessons and Takeaways

"When we stop doing our best work, our enthusiasm for the job wanes. We must motivate ourselves to do our very best and, by our example, lead others to do their best as well. People like to follow those who are excited about their work, not workaholics."

"Do the best you can every day and take advantage of unexpected opportunities. That combination will lead you to success."

Ordinary people are the worst of the best and the best of the worst. They never achieve anything unusual; they just go with the flow. Don't be average; be exceptional.

If you're excited about what you're doing, it's a lot more likely that your employees will also be excited. People want to work for a person, not a company. It's about relationships.

"We must motivate ourselves to do our very best, and by our example lead others to do their best as well."

Truett Cathy

How Did You Do It Truett?

by Truett Cathy

Truett Cathy was the founder and CEO of Chick-fil-A. He opened his first restaurant in 1946. Twenty years later he still had only one restaurant. This is the story of how Truett Cathy grew Chick-fil-A to thousands of restaurants.

His restaurants are closed on Sunday—traditionally the day most people eat out with their families. But Chick-fil-A has higher employee retention and overall profits than places open all week.

At the heart of Truett Cathy's philosophy is a proverb he memorized when he was eight years old: "A good name is rather to be chosen than great riches, and loving favor rather than silver or gold" Proverbs 22:1.

His lessons apply to business, family, and life.

Lessons and Takeaways

"The most satisfying day is the day you work the hardest, the day you get the most done. When you do less than you're capable of doing, it's work. When you do an outstanding job, it's rewarding."

When you are courteous to your employees, suppliers, and customers, when you show them you sincerely appreciate them, you create a force for good.

It's important to live by your convictions. Businesses don't succeed or fail - people do.

"When you're 100% committed to something, you're not likely to be discouraged or give up. When you're committed, strange and unusual things tend to happen to help you out. When you're 100% committed you're not likely to fail."

Truett Cathy

Self Made in America

by John McCormack

John McCormack was a New York police officer who wanted to start a business.

He realized that first-generation immigrants could teach him what it takes to win. He became a mentee to four successful immigrant business owners and used what he learned to build a huge business.

In this book, he talks about motivation, setting goals, hard work, and the American Dream.

Lessons and Takeaways

Create a personal balance sheet but focus on the positive side of your ledger. Concentrate on your strengths.

You learn very little from success, so go ahead and make mistakes; you'll find success on the other side of failure.

Worry causes doubt, and doubt causes inaction. Whenever you start worrying, focus on your dreams; they will motivate you to take action.

When in doubt, trust yourself. Go back to what feels right. Go back to what follows your values and personality.

Do whatever it takes. Your efforts today will pay off tomorrow.

"Confidence doesn't come from knowledge or theory; it comes from experience. You have to be willing to pay the price."

John McCormack

Always do more than you're paid for, and soon, you'll be paid more for what you do.

Pick your friends for their integrity, not for their money.

If you're not good at it, hire someone else to do it. Focus your time and energy on doing the things you're good at.

Once you've determined your goal, focus on it and stop wasting your time on activities that don't contribute to your goal.

"The best way to develop self-discipline is by establishing what needs to be done, assigning enough time to do it properly, setting a time to get started, and taking action."

John McCormack

About the Authors

Gracen Gonzalez is a 17 year old high school senior.

He's been homeschooled all his life and has always had an interest in building and flying aircraft. He's soloed a plane at 16 and is learning how to fly powered parachutes.

Gracen hopes to attend the U.S. Air Force Academy due to its culture of academic excellence and leadership development.

Gracen applies himself 100% to everything he does. He's a top student with a 4.21 GPA.

He's a two-time Colorado Judo Champion. He took up the sport of wrestling when he was a high school freshman. By his junior year he was team captain and wrestled in the Colorado State Tournament.

Gracen owns and operates a 3D printing and design business that sells high-quality engineering models around the world. He works part-time as a 3D printing R&D and CAD specialist. He gives presentations on 3D printing and CAD to local STEM groups.

He's been playing piano for 11 years and is a worship leader at his church. Gracen serves in youth ministry as a student leader.

LaunchPadGracen.com

Ruben Gonzalez is Gracen's proud dad.

He wasn't a gifted athlete. He didn't take up the sport of luge until he was 21.

Against all odds, four years and a few broken bones later, he was competing in the Calgary Winter Olympics. At the age of 47, at the Vancouver Olympics he became the first person to ever compete in four Winter Olympics in four different decades.

Ruben's the author of the critically acclaimed books, *The Courage to Succeed* and *The Shortcut.*

Since 2002, he's spoken for over 100 Fortune 500 companies. Ruben lives in Colorado. He enjoys hiking, sailing and flying.

Gracen's Story in Pictures

As Gracen's plane building grew from rubber-band powered
to remote-controlled planes, he needed to find a way
to fund his hobby.

His dad made him a deal. For every personal development
book Gracen read and wrote a short report listing the things
he learned, he would give Gracen $10.

Gracen read over 80 books, made $800, but best of all,
he began to apply the success and leadership principles
he learned in every part of his life.

Before long Gracen started designing his own planes and discovered that he enjoyed the engineering side of aviation.

Civil Air Patrol   Wright Flyer Simulator

Building a 3D Printer

3D Printing Presentation

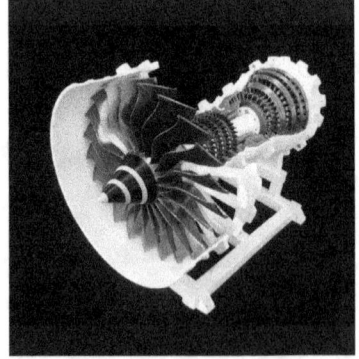

Gracen builds and sells high-quality engineering models.

He's learning to fly planes and powered parachutes.

Sports

Gracen was a member of the Olympic Training Center Judo Club for seven years. The first 18 months Gracen did judo, he didn't win a single competitive judo match. He kept at it and went on to win two Judo State Championships. He understands delayed gratification and giving yourself time to learn the skills that lead to success. Watch videos here: **LaunchPadGracen.com**

Gracen took up the sport of wrestling as a high school freshman. By his junior year he the was team captain and qualified to compete in the Colorado State Championship.

He's been playing piano for 11 years and taking singing lessons for 3 years. He was a co-winner in the Music Competition of the 2022 Summit National Conference. He's a worship leader at his church and serves in youth ministry as a student leader.

Gracen was in charge of giving the safety briefing and leading the adult participants at a local AirSoft event. Because of his natural leadership, the adults, several of whom were active military, readily followed his lead.

LaunchPadGracen.com

Praise from High Achievers

"I have known Gracen since he was 8. I have never met a more driven, talented, and intelligent young man. He has a passion for a myriad of intellectual, artistic, and athletic pursuits and excels at all of them. I have thoroughly enjoyed watching him grow into an exceptional young man and leader. His acceptance into the US Air Force Academy and subsequent service will make this country safer."

Brad Coughlin - Major US Army (Ret)
Army Ranger, Special Forces Medic, and Medical Officer

"Gracen is one of the very top students I've worked with in my decades-long education career. He has created many STEM projects, has the heart of an engineer, and is a young man of outstanding character."

Mark Hyatt - Colonel USAF (ret.), former Director of the USAFA Center for Character and Leadership Development

"Gracen is exactly the kind of high performing young man of character that we want at our Academy and as an officer in our Air Force."

Colonel Mickey Addison - Retired US Air Force

"Gracen Gonzalez is a remarkable young man. He pursues everything with all his energy and it shows in his results!"

Scott Parazynski - Former NASA Astronaut, Everest Climber, Medical Doctor

"Gracen is mentally rugged, physically strong, intellectually focused, and deeply passionate about his dreams of attending the USAFA and the contribution he'd like to make to the world. It's rare for a young person to possess such a clear, and consistent vision for themselves and then work towards that dream at such a high level and with such passion and consistency."

Bruce Babashan - USA Boxing & Pro Boxing Trainer

"The thing that stands out about Gracen, is how diverse he is in his interests and excels in a wide variety of concepts and applications for each of those interests."

Don Wilson - Mayor of Monument, Colorado

"There are certain people who you know are going to do big things in the world. They have a unique mixture of intelligence, character, personality, and grit. Gracen Gonzalez is one of those few."

Jim Harshaw Jr. - NCAA Division I Wrestling Coach and All American Wrestler

"Gracen is an outstanding young man. Focused, hard-working, multi-talented, mentally tough as nails and coachable. He will make a great Air Force Officer."

David Kimes - Olympian, 2X World Shooting Champion, Navy Wounded Warriors Shooting Coach

"I have personally seen Gracen's passion and skill for flying grow over the ten years I've known him. Gracen is dedicated, energetic, knowledgeable and fun loving. He loves helping other people."

Denver Collins - US Air Force Retired Flight Instructor

"I have known Gracen since he was born. He has always been inquisitive, diligent and perseveres in all activities in which he tackles."

Todd Guest - Co-Founder & CEO of Spirit Oil & Gas

"Gracen has an insatiable drive, curiosity and a strong, solid character of the highest caliber. He is a joy to be around and has developed through the years to become a high level contributor in life!"

D.J. Vanas - former Chief of Minority Enrollment, USAFA Admissions and USAFA graduate

"I have led many young men and women, both enlisted and officers into combat and can personally attest that Gracen has the mental, physical, and emotional courage to become an exceptional officer and future outstanding leader in the U.S. Air Force."

Robert May III - USAFA graduate (ret.) with 21+ years as a Command Pilot with over 360 combat hours in the C-130

"Gracen's unmatched drive to accomplish goals sets him well apart from his peers."

Dino Verones Jr
Sergeant Major Retired,
US Army Special Forces

"Gracen is a young leader with a passion for personal development and growth. He is driven to learn, and I cannot wait to see the heights he hits!"

Tracey C. Jones - MBA, Ph.D., Major USAF

How to Get Your Kids to Read Great Books

1 - **Make it fun**, not work.

2 - **Parable books** are short story books with lessons. They are a great way to start. *The Go-Giver, Don't Eat the MarshMallow Yet, The Fred Factor, Who Stole the Cheese, The Tiny Warrior, Rhinoceros Success*, etc.

3 - **Biographies by Pat Williams**, the General Manager of the Orlando Magic, are great because he unpacks the lessons at the end of every chapter. *21 Great Leaders, How to be Like Walt* (Disney), *How to be Like Mike* (Jordan).

4 - **Look for books that fit your child's interests.** Gracen liked anything to do with aviation and leadership, so he read a lot of those books.

5 - **It's about what they learn**; not about the report. I told Gracen that he didn't have to write a fancy report; that would have made it work. I told him that I wanted a list of the things he learned and some of his favorite quotes.

6 - **Pay them in a currency that's important to them.** Gracen wanted to earn money for his aviation hobby so I paid him $10 per book + report. If your child is interested in something else. Offer them that.

The key is to get your kids to learn success principles they can use to create a great life; to make reading books a *Launch Pad* to success.

www.ingramcontent.com/pod-product-compliance
Lightning Source LLC
Chambersburg PA
CBHW060531130626
46553CB00002B/712